THE
TRIBE HAS
SPOKEN

Life Lessons from Reality TV

DAVID VOLK

**Andrews McMeel
Publishing**

Kansas City

04 05 06 07 08 KP1 10 9 8 7 6 5 4 3 2

ISBN: 0-7407-4686-3

Library of Congress Control Number: 2004101697

To my father, Larry Volk, who would have been proud even though he may not have understood, and my mother, Lois, who made the mistake of encouraging me.

"Grab your torch. The tribe has spoken. Time for you to go."

—Jeff Probst, *Survivor*

CONTENTS

ACKNOWLEDGMENTS

No project, no matter how big or small, comes as the result of the work of just one person. While my name may go on the cover, I couldn't have done this without the support of my family and many friends. What I'm saying is, there's plenty of blame to go around.

Depending on your point of view, the other people who should be celebrated or held accountable include my wife, Cindy, who, when she wasn't busy serving our country, had to put up with my endless eight-hour days of sitting in a darkened room watching television; my brother-in-law, Andrew Hess, who suggested I interview for a job at a book packager that I did not get; for the folks at becker & mayer!, including editor Adrienne Wiley, who wisely decided that a person who is so thin probably shouldn't do a humor book on fad diets; and my editor at Andrews McMeel Publishing, Polly Blair, who has answered numerous silly questions and provided additional incentive by promising me a barbecue lunch should I ever make it back to Kansas City.

Other unindicted coconspirators include a cadre of videotape-machine owners who make President

Richard Nixon's secretary, Rose Mary Woods, look like a rank amateur when it comes to taping, erasing, and taping again. They include the members of the pub trivia team Who's Your Daddy?, Nick "Geography Boy" Fraser, Val "The Scribe" Hockens, Ann "The Movie Goddess" Hockens, Janna "The Editor-minator" Silverstein, and Gena Shapiro (who is in a class by herself). Debroa Robson and Mike Bottingfield aren't totally blameless, either. Elizabeth Davis and Rob Jacobs occasionally gave up sleep when they did late-night tapings because the sound of the VCR starting up and shutting down woke them.

Also, a special thanks to my cousin Richard Isaac, who gave me the entire run of *Boy Meets Boy*, *Real World: Seattle*, *Queer Eye for the Straight Guy*, and a season of *Amazing Race* all on tape and neatly catalogued to boot. Who knew?

One final thanks to Prudy Taylor Board, my family, and all of the subscribers to my rant list who faithfully receive and occasionally read the humor commentaries I e-mail every week or so.

INTRODUCTION

I have seen the light and it is . . . reality television.

Go ahead, scoff if you will. I, too, was once an unbeliever. Like you, I, too, once found myself wandering the globe in search of answers to all the age-old questions that have haunted the sages for years. Questions like, What is the meaning of life? Are we alone in the universe? What happens to my soul when I die? Who moved the cheese? Who put the bop in the bop she bop she bop? Who put the ram in the ram a lam a ding dong? And, even more important, will someone from the Office of Homeland Security be waiting on my doorstep if I rip the tag off my sofa pillows?

Not too surprisingly, my search took me to many of the world's centers of great thought in such mysterious cities as Jerusalem, Bangkok, Paris, Kuala Lumpur, Prague, and Rome. By day, I roamed the halls of libraries and wandered the streets in search of wisdom. And in the evening I sought out philosophers and poets in coffeehouses and bars, hoping for a few crumbs of wisdom, all to little avail.

Discouraged, I was on the second day of a fast to cleanse the impurities from my system when the answer almost dropped into my lap. I had taken a momentary break from my search for enlightenment to watch an episode of *Seinfeld* and was channel surfing between commercials when the answer hit me. I had somehow stumbled across *Cops* and sat mesmerized as I watched numerous evildoers being arrested for their individual violations of the law. Twenty minutes into the show, I noticed that every criminal had a blurred, pixilated face. And then the show's simple lesson became so obvious that I couldn't help but see: If you want to keep out of trouble, avoid people with pixilated faces. One of those lifelong questions had been answered. I thanked God that I knew how to read between the lines.

I was hooked. I had to know if all television shows had such useful lessons. I watched dramas like *Law & Order* (Lesson: We're going to catch you), *Law & Order: Special Victims Unit* (If you're a pervert, we're going to catch you), and *CSI* (We're going to use technology to catch you). I watched action shows like *Alias* (We don't know who we are, but we're going to get you). Then there were legal programs like *The Practice* (We're going to get you off) and reruns of *LA Law* (We're going to sue the pants off you). Next came sitcoms, including *Everybody Loves Raymond* (Lesson: Everybody loves Raymond), *Friends* (It's good to have friends), and *Seinfeld* (Um . . . er . . . um).

As a last resort, I hesitantly turned to reality television and was richly rewarded. "What's the lesson of *Survivor*?" you might ask. "In order to survive you must outwit, outlast, outplay, and outconnive your opponent." How about *Queer Eye for the Straight Guy*? "Gay people are our friends, not our enemies, and if you don't clean up your act pretty darn quick, you're going to lose your girlfriend." At the same time *The Simple Life* shows us that "life in the country isn't as simple as you might think, especially when you don't know what you're doing."

The lessons don't end there, though. No, the best part is that almost every episode of these unscripted shows is filled with everyday wisdom and common sense that we can use to help us live our lives. Sometimes the insights come in the form of advice to fellow participants, other times they are confessions shared only with the audience, and, occasionally, they are gems of intelligence that drop from the lips of people who suddenly appear smarter than you might think or dumber than you dared believe was possible.

The trouble with these insights is they often come so fast and furious that average audience members completely miss them. That is why I have decided to step into the fray and offer this collection of lessons distilled from the shows themselves as a public service to you.

I understand you may resist at first. You may be skeptical and find it hard to believe that so maligned an art form has so much to offer. In fact, your disbelief may continue as you read the first few lessons, but by the time you finish a section you will no doubt be slapping yourself on the knee or smacking yourself on the head and asking yourself how you missed something so obvious the first time you heard it. You may also be asking yourself how come you didn't do such a book. The answer is simple, really. I'm smarter than you are, and I thought of the idea first.

Read and learn.

From a man who's been to the top of the reality mountain and has returned to share his wisdom,

David Volk

CHILDREN

From **QUEER EYE FOR THE STRAIGHT GUY**, a show where five gay men give a complete fashion makeover to an unenlightened straight guy.

"We sold your children to pay for the furniture. I think you'll find it's a better investment in the long run."

> —Carson, to divorced father Tom M. during his makeover

Lesson: Furniture may be expensive, but at least you don't have to pay to send it to college.

From **RICH GIRLS**, which follows the daily life of designer Tommy Hilfiger's daughter, Ally, and her friends.

"I miss my childhood so much. Lately, like, even, like, for a year or two, anytime I think about or someone brings up my childhood I get a big ball in my throat, and sometimes I cry about it, you know? Do you understand how many therapists have told me how much of my childhood I have missed? I didn't go through, like, an adolescence, you know? And I think that it's, like, really starting to affect me."

> —Ally Hilfiger

Lesson: Take time out to enjoy your youth, even if you have to miss a meeting with your therapist to do it.

From **MAKEOVER STORY**, a program where deserving participants are given a style makeover.

"I dressed them alike when they were little. They were twins. They were mine. I could do what I wanted with them."

> —The mother of twins Tracy and Stacy, explaining how she chose clothes for two girls who grew up to want a complete style makeover

Lesson: While most parents realize they will become an embarrassment to their teenage children, it never hurts to get the first shot in early.

From **RICH GIRLS**.

"You know how you can have, like, just nothingness, not even anything to be upset about, you just are?"

> —A confused, angst-ridden eighteen-year-old Ally Hilfiger

Lesson: Teenagers don't need a reason to get emotional, they just do.

From **THE OSBOURNES**, a show following the comings and goings of the family of heavy metal rocker and Prince of Darkness Ozzy Osbourne.

Jack: *"Why do you still hold this grudge from six years ago, and you still get angry when we talk about it, Kelly?"*

Kelly: *"Because you f - - - ing shot me."*

Jack: *"Yeah, what's your point?"*

Lesson: Be kind to your siblings or they'll never let you live it down.

COMMON SENSE

From **THE OSBOURNES**.

After Sharon talks about getting their dogs a therapist because they appear to have regressed and are no longer housebroken, Ozzy wakes up and discovers the dogs waiting to be let out early in the morning.

"You don't need to hire a dog therapist, you need to wake up at seven A.M. and open the f - - - ing door!"

Lesson: There are times when the simple solution really is best.

From **AMERICA'S NEXT TOP MODEL**, a show in which ten women compete to become America's next supermodel.

When the girls go out for pizza and Elyse eats only oatmeal, the rest of the group becomes concerned that she has an eating disorder. Giselle decides to confront her about the issue. Elyse admitted she was annoyed but decided not to be rude.

"I'm not willing to alienate Giselle because she's the only one with a straightening iron."

Lesson: Being considerate is a good thing, especially when the person you're being nice to has what you need.

From **WHAT NOT TO WEAR**, where two style mavens help a victim of bad fashion buy a new wardrobe provided the person is willing to dump his or her old clothes and follow advice from the experts.

"If I had a dollar for every time somebody told me, 'Oh yeah, black, it's slimming.' Black is only slimming if it fits correctly. It's not just slimming on its own."

— Host Stacy, to makeover victim Ross

Lesson: A color can go only so far in making you appear slender. If you really want to look thinner, lose weight.

From **CELEBRITY MOLE YUCATAN**, a show where celebrities struggle to find the person who is sabotaging their efforts to complete tasks and raise money before they are eliminated from the competition.

"For Corbin and I to come back and try to participate in such a psychotic event must mean that the two of us are . . . psychotic people."

— Stephen Baldwin, talking about Corbin Bernsen's and his own decision to appear on the show again, despite having lost in the first celebrity installment

Lesson: If it looks like a duck, walks like a duck, and talks like a duck, it's probably a duck.

From **THE AMAZING RACE 4**.

"That was the first dagger that doesn't quite kill you, but it tells you that you better start working a little harder not to die."

> —David, on not getting a flight to Tokyo from Sydney to Honolulu, when they needed it

Lesson: If at first you don't get killed, head for cover.

From **THE SIMPLE LIFE**, a show where celebrity socialites Paris Hilton and Nicole Richie leave all the trappings of their luxurious, big city lives behind and try to prove they can survive living in a small Arkansas town.

"Here are some balloons to hang on to. If you see a kid, they like to see a balloon, not the finger."

> —Manager at a local fast-food restaurant, to Nicole and Paris, who are standing on a sidewalk, dressed

as milk shakes and making obscene gestures at people driving by the restaurant

Lesson: You'll attract more people with honey than with an obscene gesture.

From **WHAT NOT TO WEAR**.

"You're wearing these high school T-shirts as conversation starters. I think we can find another way for you to start a conversation."

—Host Stacy, criticizing David L.'s penchant for wearing ripped shorts and old high-school T-shirts even though he is in his mid-thirties

Lesson: There's nothing wrong with saying hello.

From **QUEER EYE FOR THE STRAIGHT GUY**.

"I keep everything in my pants."

—Steven S.

Lesson: There's a place for everything and everything in its place.

9

From **THE ANNA NICOLE SHOW**, the program following the life of former *Playboy* model Anna Nicole Smith.

"People asked me if I ever learned anything when I was a stripper. Yes, I did. One man plus two beers equals $20."

—Anna Nicole

Lesson: Your teachers were right—math really is important.

From **1900 HOUSE**, the Public Broadcasting System's take on reality television, where a modern British family agrees to forgo all of the modern conveniences to live in a turn-of-the-century Victorian home under the same conditions experienced by families of the era.

"It's a bit odd to have somebody in your house who isn't a member of the family but gets to look at your dirty stuff and, you know, wash up. I feel it's just a bit strange really. It doesn't feel like your own home. I feel quite . . . not uncomfortable because of her, because she's actually very nice and easy to get on with, but it's quite uncomfortable to have someone in your home that isn't a member of your family. It doesn't really come naturally to me for somebody else to be doing my cleaning up."

—Joyce, on hiring a maid

Lesson: The best way to keep your cleaning staff from going through your stuff is to clean up before they show up for work.

From **THE ANNA NICOLE SHOW**.

"Unfortunately, a Jew shouldn't be tying down a Christmas tree."

> —Howard Stern, Anna's lawyer and friend, explaining why a Christmas tree fell off the car

Lesson: Stick with what you know or bad things could happen.

From **THE OSBOURNES**.

"You don't go to someone's father, 'I don't like the redness in your hair.' It's f - - - ing rude. I would never go to her father, 'Oh, I don't like the baldness, maybe you should get a f - - - ing toupee.'"

> —Kelly, talking to a friend who has just told her dad she isn't so fond of his hair coloring

Lesson: If you don't have something nice to say, don't say anything at all.

From **THE RESTAURANT**, a show in which a celebrity chef wannabe struggles to build, staff, and open a New York City restaurant in seven and a half weeks. The night of the soft opening, the staff face a crisis when they run out of wineglasses.

"We're completely out of glass. No dishwashers. So, everybody else is going to get plastic. Except for Rocco's friends. They're not getting plastic. We're going to go wash out some glasses for them."

— Hostess

Lesson: It really is who you know.

From **NEWLYWEDS: NICK AND JESSICA**, a show following the first years of marriage for singer Jessica Simpson and her husband, Nick Lachey.

"I hate record labels. They think they know everything. I want to hear them try to sing it."

> —Jessica, frustrated over troubles she's having with her record label telling her she needs to rerecord her single because it was too bluesy and too difficult to sing along with

Lesson: Remember the golden rule: The company that puts up the gold gets to make the rules, even if you don't think they know what they are doing.

From **QUEER EYE FOR THE STRAIGHT GUY**.

"You have a very relaxed lifestyle. You work in a casual environment. You've got two educations to pay for when the little ones grow up; you don't need to be wasting your money on couture. . . . I can't believe I just said that."

> —Carson, to divorced dad Tom M. discussing his decision to focus on a casual wardrobe

Lesson: Now and then, even the most frivolous of us occasionally has a practical idea that stuns us.

From **NEWLYWEDS: NICK AND JESSICA**.

"Twenty-three is old. It's almost twenty-five, which is almost mid-twenties."

—Jessica, on her upcoming birthday

Lesson: Some people take mathematical precision way too seriously. Granted, being twenty-five isn't exactly the mid-twenties; being age twenty-five years and six months is, but that's just splitting hairs.

From **THE JOE SCHMO SHOW**, a hybrid reality show where everyone is in on the joke except for one man, Matthew Kennedy Gould. Instead of being a spontaneous, unscripted show, all but one of the participants are actors playing parts. Only one character thinks it's a real competition.

When one of the house members takes all of the photos out of a cast member's prized photo album and replaces them with pictures of his butt, a fellow cast member and war veteran, Earl, tries to put it all into perspective.

"It's not an arm and a leg in a mortar attack. It's photographs. That's all. It's photographs. Okay, it's photographs of somebody's ass."

Lesson: There's no need to take everything so seriously.

From **CLEAN SWEEP**, a show where organization experts help hapless homeowners declutter the two worst rooms in their house.

"I venture to say that you actually packed and moved a container of dried mushrooms. What was he thinking when you were packing those boxes? 'Honey, get the mushrooms? Don't forget the mushrooms and the alarm clock'?"

> —Organizer Shelli, confronting participants with an eight-year-old container of dried shiitake mushrooms

Lesson: One man's mushrooms are another man's trash.

From **THE OSBOURNES**.

"The thing about life is, by the time you get old enough to understand what it's all about, you die."

—Ozzy, during dinner

Lesson: Knowledge comes with age.

From **RICH GIRLS**.

"Fabio will not be modeling on my cover. It's going to be like a real novel."

—Jaime Gleicher, on the book she's writing

Lesson: You can judge a book by its cover.

COMMUNICATION

From **THE AMAZING RACE 4**, a show where teams use their wit, street smarts, and speed to compete against one another while completing a series of tasks in locations all over the world.

After Tian storms off at the end of an argument with her partner, Jaree, fellow contestants Kelly and Jon offer Jaree helpful advice on communicating.

"You know what I like to do? When I'm having a hard time with Jon communicating, I like to write a letter. Have you thought about writing Tian a letter? That might help," Kelly says. Jon helpfully adds, *"The title of the letter could be 'You Selfish Bitch.' Dear Tian. I just wanted to express some of my thoughts."*

Lesson: Advice is free, but really good advice is unusable.

From **SURVIVOR: THE AMAZON**, a show where sixteen contestants are left in a remote location to struggle against the elements and one another in hopes of winning $1 million by outwitting, outplaying, and outlasting their opponents.

"It is important for me to have people on my team that are going to do what I am telling them to do without knowing that I am telling them to do it."

—Rob

Lesson: A good leader should put the fun back in dysfunctional.

From **THE REAL WORLD: PARIS**, an MTV program that shows the interactions between seven people who don't know one another living together in the same house as they grow to appreciate and occasionally hate their housemates.

"With great power comes great responsibility. Who said that? I think it was in Spider-man: The Movie.*"*

—Adam, about how he's sure the United States will do the right thing if it comes to war with Iraq

Lesson: Sometimes, when words fail, the best way to express your thoughts is to quote a movie superhero. Or Yogi Berra.

From **QUEER EYE FOR THE STRAIGHT GUY**.

"Isn't it funny the conversations you have with gay guys that's so different from, like, straight friends? It's fun building bridges . . . one manicure at a time."

> —Grooming guru Kyan, to Andrew L., as they chat during the makeover victim's manicure

Lesson: If all of the gay guys and straight guys went to the same salon, what a wonderful world it would be.

From **PARADISE HOTEL**, where the goal is to stay paired up with a member of the opposite sex to avoid being sent packing.

When Keith, a particularly inscrutable player, joined the cast, the men and women alike were driven to a frenzy trying to predict his next move, prompting the men to try to pierce his mental veil.

"Keith is the hardest person to read. I'm trying to get in his mind right now without asking him."

> —Beau

Lesson: You don't have to knock before you get into someone's head.

From **_THE BACHELOR_**, a show where a bachelor dates twenty-five women in an effort to find Miss Right.

"_There's a time and place for everything and I think that whatever moments I share with you are no one else's business, just as the moments I share with them at this point are not anyone else's business, either. If I were to be asked this same question by someone else, I wouldn't feel it was appropriate for me to tell what type of moment you and I shared, if we shared any type of moment at all._"

> —Bob the Bachelor's answer to Mary's question on whether he'd been intimate with other women on the show

Lesson: It's not what you say, it's how you say it . . . even if you don't know what you just said.

From **_THE BACHELOR_**.

"_He didn't answer my question. He didn't come out and verbally say it, but when I looked in his eyes, he gave me an answer and he made me feel better._"

> —Mary, interpreting Bob's nonanswer to her question about his being intimate with other women on the show

Lesson: It's not what you hear, it's how you hear it.

From ***THE REAL WORLD: SEATTLE***.

"How do I feel about sex? It's a good thing, not a bad thing, but I mean that some people's, you know, moms tell them not to go jump in that pond, but I want to know if you're currently listening to your mom."

> —Stephen, to Oruba, his girlfriend, on the phone

Lesson: Eschew obfuscation.

From ***THE REAL WORLD: PARIS***.

While hanging out at a restaurant in Florence, Italy, Adam, Ace, and Chris talk about their other housemates. Talk eventually turns to the subject of Simon, the only gay housemate.

"I would love to hang out with Simon if he didn't shop so damn much. It always comes back to shopping or some name-brand piece of clothing."

Lesson: The best way to communicate with someone is to find a common ground. If you don't like shopping and he doesn't like sports, you can always talk about your feelings. Then again, maybe not.

COPING WITH ILLNESS

From **THE REAL WORLD: SEATTLE**.

When David's friend Anthony visits, Lindsay is impressed with how well adjusted he is, considering he has spinal cancer.

"You like being around Anthony. He has such a positive outlook on things. It's just unfortunate you get that outlook battling something like cancer."

Lesson: Nothing earns you respect like smiling in the face of cancer.

From **THE REAL WORLD: SEATTLE**.

"This is not something I want to be going through right now, you know what I mean? And I don't want to be talking about it. I don't want to be sick right now."

— Irene, talking about a mysterious illness that turns out to be a relapse of Lyme disease

Lesson: Plan ahead. Getting sick is so inconvenient.

From **THE REAL WORLD: SEATTLE**.

"You've got to know that if you're sick and you want sympathy, you better, like, be sympathetic to other people first because I'll be the first one to turn you off."

> —Stephen, telling Irene why he is still angry
> with her behavior toward him while she was
> suffering a relapse of Lyme disease

Lesson: The best way to ensure that people will be kind to you in your hour of need is to make sure that you show concern about their problems in between bouts of vomiting.

From **RICH GIRLS**.

"I am not going to do anything to hurt myself or suicide. Who would take care of my dogs? Sam would be waiting at the door for the rest of his life. I couldn't do that to him. How could I do that to him? He was abandoned once already."

> —Sheila Gleicher, on why she isn't hopeless
> even though she has multiple sclerosis

Lesson: It's important to have a reason to live, even if it isn't one of your children.

CULTURAL
EXPERIENCES

From **THE SIMPLE LIFE**.

"So, you've never been on a dairy farm? You don't like the odor, I can tell. That's not near as bad as the perfume you've got on."

> —Danny, the owner of the dairy farm where Nicole and Paris work, as the two women report for work an hour late

Lesson: Smell is in the nose of the beholder.

From **I'M WITH BUSEY**, a short-lived show where Gary Busey fan Adam follows the movie star around and learns about life.

"If we get splattered with blood, that's an honor. One day I went to an ultimate fighting contest. I got splattered with so much blood in my face by Ken Shamrock in the tank that I looked like I had smallpox, but I was proud to wear it."

> —Gary

Lesson: What may be an honor to you may be completely disgusting to someone else.

From **THE AMAZING RACE 4**.

"Eating those octopus, octopi, was not culturally broadening because I could have eaten one and gotten the taste. They gave us an entire plate of live, wiggling octopi. It was awful."

> —Chip, after being the unlucky teammate
> who had to choke down a delicacy that was
> still moving

Lesson: Bad food is not culturally enriching, even if there's plenty of it.

From **THE SIMPLE LIFE**.

"Don't you guys get bored of making, like, squares? You guys should make it, like, a little edgier, you know? Like, maybe, like, some cigarette burns."

> —Nicole, speaking to a quilting group making
> traditional quilts for sale

Lesson: That tradition stuff is so over.

29

From **THE REAL WORLD: SEATTLE**.

"This man was doing things I've never seen done before and I probably never will see done again and he's doing them with his penis."

>—Lindsay, recalling one of the strangest things she saw in Nepal

Lesson: Amazing feats and awe-inspiring stunts are even more impressive when done with your penis.

From **THE REAL WORLD: PARIS**.

"You talk about your first experiences. I'm going to the strip club with four girls and a gay guy and no money; that's a first. That's like going to the fair without any tickets."

>—Ace, preparing for a cheap night on the town

Lesson: Money can't buy happiness, but it sure can help fund an evening's worth of fun.

DATING AND RELATIONSHIPS

From **QUEER EYE FOR THE STRAIGHT GUY**.

"Kids are great accessories, and everyone looks good with them. They're a great women magnet."

> —Style maven Carson, to makeover subject and divorced dad Tom M. during a visit to a clothing store

Lesson: If you want to pick up a babe, pick up a baby.

From **THE REAL WORLD: SEATTLE**.

Although Janet has had a few dates with one of David's coworkers, she's not quite sure what to make of her feelings when the guy keeps calling.

"I'm used to chasing after guys who aren't into me when I'm into them. This is the first time when I'm into someone and having them into me is kind of weird, you know what I mean? I just . . . I've got to figure things out. I'll talk to you soon."

Lesson: If you're interested in a person who is also interested in you, there's either something wrong with you, the other person, or both of you.

From **AVERAGE JOE**, where average-looking men compete to win the heart of a beautiful girl who thought she was going to be choosing from a cast of hunky guys.

"I know I could be an amazing catch. Personally, I'm dying for female attention at this point. I like being able to be discovered. I feel like I haven't really been discovered by the right woman yet."

> —Walter, on dating

Lesson: If you're looking for the perfect mate, you can't sit back and wait to be discovered. You may be a big guy, but if it took America hundreds of years to be discovered, you don't stand a chance.

From **AVERAGE JOE**.

"I know there's somebody out there that deserves me and is going to be exactly what I need and want."

> —Walter, on his hopes for the show and his romantic future

Lesson: Even if the odds are against you, it never hurts to hope.

From **THE BACHELOR**.

When Bob and Mary meet for their final date, they have this exchange.

"I'm thinking maybe I should take off my clothes."

—Mary

"I like your style."

—Bob

Lesson: The quickest way to a man's heart is through a woman's clothes.

From **THE BACHELOR: THE WOMEN TELL ALL**, a reunion show featuring interviews with women Bob the Bachelor didn't pick.

"Why did you go into detail about the children? I think once you get him wrapped around your finger you could do that, but you can't do that prior, honey."

—Lanah, asking Mary why she told Bob she wanted to start having kids shortly after a wedding, if they got married

Lesson: Honesty may be the best policy, but not when it really matters.

From **BOY MEETS BOY**, a dating program where a gay man must choose his perfect man from a field of fifteen and doesn't know some of them are straight.

"Obviously, I'm here for James, but now that Dan is gone, I miss him. I don't know if Dan feels the same way, but if he doesn't I will stalk him until he does."

> —Bryan, on his feelings for another bachelor

Lesson: If you care for someone, let them go. If they come back to you, they were yours. If they don't, you're just not trying hard enough.

From **BOY MEETS BOY**.

"I'm so excited to see my girlfriend, to kiss my girlfriend, to tell her I love her."

> —Sean, a straight guy, on what he planned to do after being eliminated from the competition

Lesson: There's nothing like spending the month with a bunch of gay men, to make you appreciate your girlfriend.

From **THE REAL WORLD: SEATTLE**.

"I've been mentally intimate with more guys than I think any of their girlfriends have been, you know, 'cause I can get close to people."

> —Irene to Janet, as she confesses she hasn't had any boyfriends

Lesson: You can sleep with just about anyone you want, but it takes a real special person to screw with your head.

From **THE AMAZING RACE**.

"I still love him, but I don't think it's going to work. Like I said, I'm too competitive. It's not so much about the game. He seems to think it's about the game, but it's about so much more than that to me. The money was not an issue. It was giving 120 percent every single minute and that meant a lot to me, and I feel like I did it, and I feel like he didn't."

> —Lenny's girlfriend, Karyn, after she and her boyfriend came in last and were eliminated from the game

Lesson: A guy may look good on paper, but it's not always obvious that he's not up to facing the challenges that life has to offer. Sometimes you need to trek across the world to realize that your boyfriend's a quitter.

From **BOY MEETS BOY**.

"This was the second massage I've ever received in my life, the first one being in Budapest by a very large gentleman who spoke absolutely no English and rubbed me down like someone salting a leg of ham."

— Franklin, a contestant

Lesson: While it may be romantic to share a massage and a steak dinner, it isn't so romantic to be treated like a piece of meat.

From **AVERAGE JOE**.

"I just want to give Jason advice. You don't have to fill the

table with drinks to get a girl to open up with you, especially this girl."

> —Malena, after Jason orders two drinks for her and himself on their last date

Lesson: Candy may be dandy, but liquor isn't always a quicker way to get the girl—especially if the girl sees what you are doing.

From **THE AMAZING RACE 4**.

"We haven't been in a romantic involvement on this race, because I wasn't traveling forty thousand miles for sex."

> —Russell, commenting on his relationship with Cindy

Lesson: Some people just don't understand romance.

From **NEWLYWEDS: NICK AND JESSICA**.

"I made a deal with her. I said, if you cook, then I'll be the

one to do the dishes. Well, so she'd have a bowl of cereal and leave the dish in the sink."

—Nick, about his wife's cooking habits

Lesson: When you make a deal to split chores with a spouse, make sure you read the fine print first.

From **NEWLYWEDS: NICK AND JESSICA**.

Nick: *"It's like the words come out of my mouth and they never make it to her ear, some mysterious force that intercepts them."*

Brother: *"Yes, it's called a marriage certificate."*

—Nick, in frustration when his wife ignores what he has just said and begins talking as if he hasn't just asked a question

Lesson: In marriage, no one can hear you speak, let alone scream.

From **THE ANNA NICOLE SHOW**.

"They can get their own dates, but it's easier to outsource it."

> —Patti Stanger, Millionaire's Club match-
> maker, to Anna Nicole

Lesson: Blind dates are so much easier if you think of them as a job interview. With interesting fringe benefits.

From **A VERY QUEER EYE HOLIDAY**, a holiday reunion show where *Queer Eye* cast members bring back their favorite makeover victims to see if they are still following the advice they were given.

"Spa treatments are expensive, but do you know what's more expensive? Divorce."

> —Carson, to makeover survivor Adam

Lesson: An occasional massage may put a temporary dent in your wallet, but divorce goes on and on.

From **THE REAL WORLD: PARIS**.

"Sick of buying dinner and not getting a kiss, sick of moving in and her dodging my lips, sick of being fun, wish I was a jerk, 'cause I guess that nice-guy shit don't work. I'm angry right now, and I don't know why."

> —Adam, after being rejected by Stephanie, a woman he has gone out with several times and spent a great deal of money on during their dates.

Lesson: It's sad, but true. Even nice guys who pay for dinner out are hoping for dessert in.

From **PUNK'D**, on which the host and staff play practical jokes on famous people and record their reactions.

"Advice to all women: Never compliment the ex-boyfriend. I don't care if you were dating Jesus Christ's brother, Ricky Christ, he wasn't a good guy, that's what you say."

> —Host Ashton Kutscher on the etiquette of dating

Lesson: When you're out on a date, it's bad form to talk about your ex.

From **THE REAL WORLD: PARIS**.

"Kate is coming this week, and I need it because the room-mates in the house are getting hotter and hotter. By God, Simon is starting to look good to me. I need to see my girlfriend."

> —Ace, about the impending arrival of his girl-friend and the long sexual dry spell since the last time he saw her

Lesson: If you can't be with the one you love, try not to mount the next living creature that walks in the room.

From **THE REAL WORLD: SEATTLE**.

"Girls have a funny way of making you say yes. Like the waitresses at a strip club will always make you buy a drink."

> —David, talking about a woman's wiles

Lesson: A man will do anything for a woman if there's a realistic chance she's about to pull off her clothes.

From **THE REAL WORLD: PARIS**.

"I really don't mind gay guys. Most gay guys are all really good-looking. Why'd you want that for competition?"

> —Ace, talking about his gay housemate,
> Simon, and gay men in general

Lesson: Instead of being threatened by attractive gay men, straight guys should be thankful.

From **THE ANNA NICOLE SHOW**.

"I've been thinking about the differences between men and women. Women may fake orgasms, but men can fake whole relationships."

> —Anna Nicole

Lesson: Women may occasionally be dishonest, but men are real dogs.

From **THE BACHELOR**.

"Being a bachelor is a tough job, let me tell you, but some-body's got to do it. Thank God it's me."

> —Bob the Bachelor, on how difficult everyday
> life can be

Lesson: Not everyone is up to the task of dating thirteen women at once, but those of us who are willingly make the sacrifice for the rest of you.

FAMILIES KNOW BEST

From **THE OSBOURNES**.

"It's very hard for me to walk into a classroom every day when I went and be verbally abused or made fun of. They still can't get over the fact even though it happened twenty years ago that Dad bit the head off a bat. It's not fair. I don't like it."

> —Kelly, about the difficulty of being treated differently from other people because Ozzy was her dad

Lesson: The sins of the parents will be visited on their children, especially when the sins are downright stupid.

From **WHO WANTS TO MARRY MY DAD?** where four grown children get to pick their father's next wife. After one of the contestants admits to the dad that she's falling in love with him, he urges his children to throw her off the show because he's more interested in a woman they don't like and are considering voting out. His children promptly ignore his request and keep the woman he dislikes.

"I can't believe they eliminated her. My kids now in their mind are really looking out for me, but I feel like they're sort of going against me."

Lesson: Be good to your children because they may get to choose not only your nursing home but also who you marry.

From **WHO WANTS TO MARRY MY DAD?**

"It wasn't really hard to go against Dad's wishes because I don't think he's seeing the whole picture like we are. He trusts us, and I think we made the right decision."

—Karla, on why the children eliminated a
woman their father was interested in

Lesson: Children never outgrow the feeling that they know everything.

From **ONE BAD TRIP**, the MTV show that sends people who love to party to lose their inhibitions at some of the world's top party spots, then secretly invites disguised loved ones along to watch what happens. In an episode focusing on a man named Doug, Doug's sister joined her parents on the trip, and they were revolted by what they saw.

"I wanted to be here because Mom and Dad don't even know the half of what you do when you're out. So it was about time that you got uncovered and they found out I really should be the favorite child."

Lesson: You're not just imagining things. Mom really did like him better.

From **THE RESTAURANT**.

"Okay, so the soft launch didn't go as well as we'd hoped and we only had, like, a half a day to make corrections. So, I just pull out my secret weapon: my mother."

—Chef/owner Rocco Dispirito

Lesson: You're never too old to run crying to Mom.

From **THE OSBOURNES**.

"I don't know what a typical American family is because it's not abnormal to me the way I live because I live that way."

—Ozzy, reflecting on family life

Lesson: No matter how odd your family is, if you've never known anything different, then it's normal to you.

From **THE OSBOURNES**.

"I f---ing hate Christmas. Let's sit at a table with your family and see how long you can sit there without arguing about the stupidest shit."

    —Kelly

Lesson: Even families of the rich and famous hate the holidays.

From **THE OSBOURNES**.

"We've known about your dope situation for a long time, you know. Don't you think I know what it means when you order a pizza at f---ing twelve o'clock at night."

    —Ozzy, to his son, Jack, about the boy's drug problem

Lesson: No matter how hard you try, you can't fool your parents.

From **THE REAL WORLD: SEATTLE**.

"I thought I was pregnant. If the doctor tells you he thinks you're pregnant, you're pregnant. It's pretty funny because I'm a virgin. It was, like, 'Oh my God, Jesus is inside of Irene' is what I was thinking."

> —Irene, recalling how a doctor misdiagnosed
> her first bout with Lyme disease

Lesson: Immaculate conception is always the most likely explanation.

From **THE OSBOURNES**.

Sharon: *"I love Christmas. I love the whole buildup. We can all eat together, give each other our gifts, and then the kids can go out and do what they want to do and Ozzy and I can stay in with the dogs and the cats and just have a nice, quiet evening."*

Ozzy: *"You can keep on f---ing wishing, 'cause it ain't gonna be."*

Sharon: *"I know. Everybody's gonna fight, call each other bastards, and everybody will go to bed early."*

—Sharon and Ozzy, on Christmas

Lesson: It's nice to have a dream as long you don't live in a fantasy world.

From **THE OSBOURNES**.

"But, darling, let me explain something to you, you have not been standing in front of 30 billion decibels for thirty-five years. Write me a note."

—Ozzy, in response to his daughter's complaints that he couldn't hear her

Lesson: When it comes to figuring out what you're doing when they can't see you, your parents have superhuman powers, but if you disrespectfully mumble quietly enough, you might be able to get away with mildly pissing them off despite having called them a nasty name. Especially if they're rock stars.

FOOD

From **NEWLYWEDS: NICK AND JESSICA**.

"Is this chicken, what I have, or is this fish? I know this is tuna, but it says chicken. By the sea. Is that stupid? What? Don't make fun of me right now. I'm not in the mood."

> —Jessica, while eating on the couch as her
> husband watches television

Lesson: You can't always believe what you read.

From **QUEER EYE FOR THE STRAIGHT GUY**.

"It's not quiche. It's an Italian quiche. It's a manly quiche. It's a quiche with balls."

> —Ted, explaining what a torta is to makeover
> victim John V.

Lesson: Nothing helps change a person's preconceived notions toward something he's never tried like putting it in terms he understands.

From **THE REAL WORLD: SEATTLE**.

"The people in Nepal have got it all mixed up. They should worship the water buffalo because it tastes like poo and eat the cow because it's good."

—Nathan, after eating something new in
Nepal

Lesson: Taste is an acquired taste.

From **QUEER EYE FOR THE STRAIGHT GUY**.

"Have you ever taken a woman on a date where you're teaching them to shoot pool, or something where you're sort of teaching them how to do something? Even if you both flub it up, it's fun. Plus you're sort of caressing and fondling, and you've got raw fish involved."

—Food expert Ted, to a divorced dad about
the advantage of a sushi-making date

Lesson: There's nothing sexier than uncooked seafood.

From **THE ANNA NICOLE SHOW**.

"What kind of restaurant that serves steak doesn't bring you A-1 sauce?"

> —Anna Nicole, while leaving a Japanese restaurant

Lesson: If you go to a restaurant that doesn't serve your favorite sauce, you shouldn't go back.

From **QUEER EYE FOR THE STRAIGHT GUY**.

"These are uncertain times."

> —Josh D., defending the food in his house

"Not uncertain enough to eat salmon out of a can."

> —Food expert Ted

Lesson: Even in the midst of a threat of nuclear holocaust, terrorism, and rioting in the streets, gourmet food shouldn't come in a can.

FRIENDS

From **THE ANNA NICOLE SHOW**.

"There's three reasons that I like dogs better than I like men: Dogs are loyal, dogs are affectionate, and dogs can be fixed."

—Anna Nicole

Lesson: Dogs are a woman's best friend, too.

From **RICH GIRLS**.

"This girl tries to, like, act really tough and she's a sweetheart to everyone, but it's just kind of scary because she is so nice and you never really know she's, like, actually human because she doesn't express her emotions and you don't know when she is hurting even though she really is deep down inside."

—Ally Hilfiger, after telling her friend Liz that she can't go to Greece

Lesson: Nice people have feelings, too.

From **THE AMAZING RACE**.

"I won't let him in my apartment, really, because I don't, like, have friends over to the apartment, because they come in, they don't take their shoes off, they walk all over, they make a mess."

—Drew, on his best friend and teammate

Lesson: Real friends help wipe their feet.

From **THE ANNA NICOLE SHOW**.

"You know what's really important in life? It's not money, it's not what money can buy, it's friends. . . . Howard, will you bring me my f - - - ing soda?"

—Anna Nicole

Lesson: It's good to have friends, but it's even better to have your own people.

From **RICH GIRLS**.

"This guy is, like, he's, like, my friend. Like seriously. I, like, talk to him."

> —Ally Hilfiger, on the voice on the directional system in her car

Lesson: It's better to have an imaginary albeit useful friend than no friends at all.

From **1900 HOUSE**.

"I like the idea of someone waiting on me. It makes me feel important."

> —Joe

Lesson: People who have people are the luckiest people in the world.

HEALTH AND BEAUTY

From ***1900 HOUSE***.

"My hair's chosen not to have a 1900 experience, and I'm sorry. My feelings are valid, and if they don't suit other people, then hard cheese."

> —Joyce, on how turn-of-the-century methods of washing hair have turned her head into a mess

Lesson: Just because you've chosen to change your lifestyle doesn't mean that your hair will play along.

From ***THE REAL WORLD: SEATTLE***.

"Do you hear that? That's my hair. My hair is upset. The moisture just creeps through every orifice of this house. Even Paul doesn't work in extreme situations like this. Paul Mitchell, that is. Paul's my boyfriend. He's my regular man."

> —Irene, on the effect living in Seattle is having on her hair

Lesson: There's nothing worse than having someone desert you on a bad hair day.

From **QUEER EYE FOR THE STRAIGHT GUY**.

"It's kind of like a guardian angel. I never see it, but I know it's there."

> —Andrew L., on why he refuses to shave his back hair despite his girlfriend's repeated requests for him to do so

Lesson: Not everything that you can't see is good. Take unsightly back hair. It may be protecting you . . . from getting dates.

From **THE OSBOURNES**.

"Mom, Aimee wears a thong every single day and right now, she is wearing a thong of mine. So, it's been up my crack and now it's up her crack, and I'm okay with that."

> —Kelly, on thongs

Lesson: Children have different hygiene standards than adults.

INTELLIGENCE

From **THE AMAZING RACE 4**.

"I can't believe it we made it this far. This freaks me out, because, not only do I think we don't deserve to be here because we're so stupid, but I also think that it's so surreal. There's an actual million-dollar pot at the end."

> —Kelly, on the realization that she and her boyfriend are among the final three teams vying for a million-dollar prize

Lesson: Slow but steady may win the race, but stupid and greedy may not necessarily disqualify you.

From **THE ANNA NICOLE SHOW**.

"A man asked me once what I knew about cars. I don't know nothing about power steering, radiators, or crank shafts, but I know everything there is to know about back-seats."

> —Anna Nicole

Lesson: If you can't know it all, it's important to develop special areas of expertise.

From **THE AMAZING RACE 2**.

"I realized that anybody can make a mistake, anybody can make a bad decision, but to make such a catastrophically, unfathomably bad decision, it takes true imagination. It takes true determination. It proves . . . I think it proves that we're complete morons. We think, we think we're actually smart. We think we're having effective, logical strategy, whatever, when we're actually being complete morons. And so, when I realized this, it was incredibly liberating. I realized that we were morons, and it was okay. We may not have smarts. We may not have looks, well, you know, but we have heart. We have heart and you know what? Tortoises aren't smart, but tortoises win the race."

> —Gary, after realizing that what he thought was a shortcut would actually cost his team valuable time in the race

Lesson: Embrace the moron within.

From **THE REAL WORLD: SEATTLE**.

"The elephants know how to wash. They don't need our help, but I didn't think about that before it came time to wash elephants."

> —Irene, after realizing the gang was the victim of a real-life elephant joke

Lesson: Sometimes, the only way to learn how ridiculous an idea is, is to be on the receiving end of a hard lesson.

From **BOY MEETS BOY**.

"And what do I get? To be made an asshole of on national television? For caring about these people? For having somebody f---ing fool me? That's fabulous."

> —Andra, the star's gal pal, on being told that one of the remaining contestants on the show is actually straight

Lesson: If a television executive offers to put you up in a beautiful mansion, there's always a catch.

From **THE ANNA NICOLE SHOW**.

While watching the news, Anna Nicole sees stories about tensions between the Israelis and Palestinians, which prompts her lawyer to suggest she speak out in favor of Israel. Anna wisely opts out.

"I'm just going to shut up. I know nothing about nothing. Oh yes. Oh yes."

Lesson: It's better to be thought a fool than to speak up and remove all doubt.

From **FAKING IT**, a BBC program where an individual has twenty-eight days to gain enough skills from a new profession to be able to fool a panel of experts in the field.

When an art expert takes Paul, a house painter and conceptual artist wannabe, on a tour of galleries, he admits to having trouble considering some things works of art.

"To me, it's not a sculpture, it's just a bag of air. It doesn't serve a purpose. I mean, I'm totally open to my mind being changed, but at this time I think I speak for the masses when I say, 'What's this about?'"

Lesson: Minds are like parachutes. They operate best when open.

LOVE

From **QUEER EYE FOR THE STRAIGHT GUY**.

"I'd do anything for her, like staying with five gay men."

> —Port Authority policeman John V., during his makeover

Lesson: When it's true love, no sacrifice is too great.

From **THE REAL WORLD: SEATTLE**.

"I'm telling you, when you stole my heart, you stole my sexual desire and it sucks."

> —David, on a pay phone, to a mystery woman on the other end of the line

Lesson: Any guy will tell you, it's more important to have your libido than your heart because if you give away your heart, you can still get it up. But if you give away your libido . . .

From **THE NEXT JOE MILLIONAIRE**, a program where women compete to win the heart of a Texas cowboy who they think is a millionaire. The twist: He's poorer than dirt.

"I thought that I might be gone because I was cursing, I was drinking vodka, and I didn't wear any underwear."

>—Tereza, on why she was eliminated in favor of a woman David liked more

Lesson: Sometimes, habits that guys may love still aren't enough to overcome true love.

From **AVERAGE JOE**.

"Given that I've studied science and logic all my life to be in a situation where I'm possibly falling for a girl on the first date is beyond any calculation that I possibly could fathom."

>—University professor Tareq

Lesson: Love doesn't play by the rules.

From **THE REAL WORLD: PARIS**.

"Am I in love with Giuseppe? No, because that takes time. Do I love the attention I get from him? Yes, and I definitely love the way he makes me feel like when he walks into a room. I feel better."

> —Leah, after a phone conversation with Giuseppe, a man she met in Italy who is wild about her

Lesson: Loving someone takes time, but enjoying a person basking in the wonderfulness that is you takes no effort at all.

From **AVERAGE JOE**.

"Some days I wake up and I'm really into Malena. All I can do is think about it. Other times it's the sport of playing with other guys' heads that gets me through the day. And the guys are ripe for the picking."

> —Zach

Lesson: Absence may make the heart grow fonder, but it never hurts to have a hobby to keep yourself busy.

MISFORTUNE

From **THE RESTAURANT**.

If he didn't already know it before, Pete discovered how cruel restaurant life can be when he didn't get the table he wanted to wait on.

"Dude, how does the gay guy get the table with seven girls? I don't understand that. I can't believe they gave you that table."

Lesson: No one ever said life was fair.

From **BIG BROTHER 2**, where participants live in the same house as they try to keep from being voted out all while trying to be the last resident remaining.

"Sue was telling me that one time it was really hot and to cool off they had to go into the ocean and it just really stung them because they had little cuts. Well, one time I had a blister on my foot playing basketball and I was in the hot tub and it was too warm so I had to move to the pool."

> —Will, comparing the deprivation of *Survivor* with the difficulties faced by competitors in *Big Brother*

Lesson: Every place has its challenges, but a true winner finds a way to overcome the difficulties.

From **THE ANNA NICOLE SHOW**.

"You know those bumper stickers where it says 'Shit happens and then you die'? They should have them where shit happens and then you live because that's really the truth of it."

—Anna Nicole, watching the news

Lesson: Life sucks.

From **1900 HOUSE**.

"I've got to go and put my corset on and don't want to. What I want to put on today is a pair of trousers and a fleece and a pair of deck shoes, but I've got to go and put on some bloody fancy dress."

—Joyce, preparing to put on a corset

Lesson: We don't always get to do what we want.

From **1900 HOUSE**.

"I am getting a raw deal. As the female, I am getting much more to put up with. He started saying he didn't know

how to shave and wasn't it sad, and oh dear he cut his face and he was given all sorts of things, beautiful perfumed lotions and potions to put on his face and enable him to have a smooth shave. It's a male thing, isn't it? I'm the one coming off worse. It's been a baptism of fire for me. I am jealous. I am jealous that he walks out of the door and goes to work. And, I suppose I am jealous because he's a man and whether it's 1900 or 1999 he gets the better deal, but I get the freer drawers."

> —Joyce, complaining that her role as a
> Victorian-era housewife is much more diffi-
> cult than the role of her husband

Lesson: Women really do get the short end of the stick.

From *THE AMAZING RACE 4*.

"We are behind the biggest loser who's ever driven a car. This guy will not let us go by him."

> —Chip, on the finale in Hawaii, as he's trying
> to pass the car ahead of him

Lesson: If the person ahead of you is slowing you down, he's a big idiot, but if you're ahead of everyone else and slowing them down . . . well, that's just good strategy.

RULES TO
LIVE BY

From **THE REAL WORLD: SAN FRANCISCO**.

"This is the first impression you want to make on everyone. 'Hi, how you doing? I've got the single, that one's mine'? I just didn't think it was the best way to meet everyone. Let's shake hands and exchange names first, then we'll decide on how we're going to screw each other over."

> —Judd, on Rachel's decision to take the only single room because she was the first person in the house

Lesson: It's always best to get to know people before you set out to screw them—that way, you can be so much more effective.

From **THE NEXT JOE MILLIONAIRE**.

"These European girls, they're not afraid to ask you, 'Well, how did you get the $80 million?' They keep hammering on it a little bit."

> —David, the millionaire

Lesson: It always pays to look as if you know what you're doing, even if you don't. Otherwise, people may begin to ask questions.

From **THE AMAZING RACE**.

"Nothing's free, Kevin. We're into Africa. You go to the Statue of Liberty, is the guy giving these things away for free? For crying out loud, free."

> —Kevin, to his fraternity brother Drew, on the map they just bought even though they don't have much money to spend

Lesson: There's no such thing as a free map. Give a person directions, he will drive for a day. Give him a map, he will drive for life.

From **QUEER EYE FOR THE STRAIGHT GUY**.

"Everyone off the dance floor. We have some white people that need to dance."

> —Grooming guru Kyan, watching Ross M. hit the dance floor at a salsa club with his girlfriend after having had only one dance lesson

Lesson: It's always best to clear the floor before inexperienced people dance for the first time. That way, no one gets hurt.

From **WHAT NOT TO WEAR: BBC**, the show where two style mavens give a hapless victim of bad fashion money to buy new clothes if the person agrees to give up the old wardrobe and follow their advice.

"Men just because they're men doesn't mean they shouldn't wear attractive underwear."

> —Hostess Trinny, upon seeing video of a man they are about to make over, wearing old, tired boxers

Lesson: Always make sure your underwear is clean and fashionable. You never know when you'll be involved in a fashion accident.

From **THE REAL WORLD: PARIS**.

"Ace didn't come here to make fun of anybody. He came to have a good time. And when other people are mocking your good time, it's going to make you angry."

> —Adam, on Ace's experience at a strip club with some of the other roommates

Lesson: It's bad form to poke fun at another person's entertainment, especially if you've invited yourself along for the ride.

From **THE SIMPLE LIFE**.

"I thought being cochair meant we wouldn't have to do a lot of work. It means the exact opposite."

> —Nicole, complaining about the amount of work involved in being honorary cochair of the town's spring festival while she's being dragged out of a nearby bar—again

Lesson: If you don't like extra work, don't volunteer.

From **THE AMAZING RACE**.

"Our stupidity is getting better. Yeah, because yesterday we were lost for three hours. Today it took us only two hours fifteen minutes."

> —Kim, on her team's ability to stay in the race

Lesson: The best way to grow is to learn from your mistakes.

From **AVERAGE JOE 2: HAWAII**.

"Phuc's all right. Phuc's a Boston kid. Phuc can open a beer bottle with his teeth. This kid's the most valuable guy we have here."

>—Brian, talking about why he likes his housemate Phuc

Lesson: People appreciate having friends with useful survival skills in case of an emergency.

From **THE SIMPLE LIFE**.

"This is the one thing we thought they could do without making a scene, and apparently, we was wrong. Do you think anybody in town's going to talk to us again?"

>—Albert, on Paris and Nicole's ability to find a way to botch their jobs as honorary cochairs of a spring festival in Altus, Arkansas

Lesson: You are judged by the company you keep.

From **QUEER EYE FOR THE STRAIGHT GUY**.

"Remember when you told me that you'd make out with me if I got you a flat-screen TV? Pucker up, baby."

> —Thom, designer, to Ross M., coming into his newly restyled apartment

Lesson: Don't make promises you're not prepared to keep.

From **WHAT NOT TO WEAR**.

"I can't handle the button fly. We're going to have to go see if they have zippers here. I couldn't wear these out drinking. If I had to do that twelve times a night, forget it."

> —Dave H., getting frustrated over his inability to fasten the fly of a pair of Armani jeans he is trying on

Lesson: Above all else, fashion should be practical.

From **THE AMAZING RACE 2**.

"We will make enemies and we will play sly when we have to. Right now, we know we don't have to. We're just going to cruise along until the decisions have to be made."

> —Alex, on his strategy in the early phase of the game

Lesson: Don't do unto others until they do unto you.

From **FRATERNITY LIFE**, an MTV show about living in a chapter house at a major university.

"I'm not really pissed that Conrad ratted us out for drinking. I'm extremely pissed that they said they wouldn't rat us out, then ratted us out anyways."

> —Earl

Lesson: Tattling is bad, but breaking a promise is even worse.

From **THE OSBOURNES**.

"If you want any advice from me about tattoos, be somebody unique. Don't have a tattoo 'cause everybody and their friend has got tattoos."

> —Ozzy, after learning that his daughter had gotten a tattoo

Lesson: Just because your friend jumped off a bridge doesn't mean you have to.

From **THE JOE SCHMO SHOW**.

During one game, the housemates are told that they will each win a television if each of them eats a fake delicacy from another country, each more disgusting than the last, until a pile of fake dog poop is put in front of the star, Matthew.

"I'm willing to forfeit everybody's television sets. I said that. If I don't eat the dog feces, then they don't get their TVs."

> —Matthew, to fake television executive after refusing to take any crap

Lesson: Be prepared to accept the consequences of your actions.

From **WHAT NOT TO WEAR**.

"You would think that an actor would know you would have to look the part sometimes to get the part. And the only part he's going to get is unemployed gay surf trash."

> —Host Clinton, on guest David L.'s lack of fashion sense

Lesson: Dress for success.

From **THE SIMPLE LIFE**.

"We're nice girls no matter whatever you heard."

> —Nicole, introducing herself to a group of women in a church quilting group

Lesson: The best defense is a good offense.

From **THE REAL WORLD: SEATTLE**.

The day after Steven slapped Irene as she left the show, everyone at the radio station where the gang works talked about what happened, and Rebecca says he deserved to feel like an outcast.

"There's definitely a stigma attached to him now that he's not going to be able to wear off and it's not a good stigma. But when you make a mistake, you're going to pay for it."

Lesson: If you have to have a stigma, make sure it's a good one.

From **THE ANNA NICOLE SHOW**.

"The New York reporters are crazy. One asked me how I became such a good lover. I told him, a lot of practice . . . on myself."

— Anna Nicole, on a New York publicity tour

Lesson: Practice makes perfect.

From **THE ANNA NICOLE SHOW**.

"I didn't get to masturbate this morning, and I've been dying to, so I've gotta go."

— Anna Nicole

Lesson: It's important to launch a rigorous exercise schedule and stick with it.

From **THE SIMPLE LIFE**.

"He's sweet. We should have a threesome with him. Let him have something."

> —Nicole, on her host family's son Justin after he has gotten up to leave an evening conversation

Lesson: Give of yourself. Even if you aren't all that attractive, it's still the thought that counts.

From **THE NEXT JOE MILLIONAIRE**.

"My dog, my horse, my girlfriend. It doesn't get no better than this."

> —David, taking stock of his few possessions after the woman he told he loved came back to him

Lesson: Sometimes the simple pleasures in life are the best . . . until the girlfriend gets jealous of the horse.

SELF-IMAGE

From **AVERAGE JOE**.

"My first impression when I came to this house was, 'I'm probably in the wrong place.' Do I want to be the best of the average? I don't know."

> —Zach, on learning he was considered an average Joe

Lesson: Don't sell yourself short. Always try to be the best of the best. But if that doesn't work, it's better to be the best of the average than the worst of the best.

From **BOY MEETS BOY**.

"I feel a little bit rejected, despite my sexual orientation. You still want to be wanted. I was trying to be sincere with James, because I was still interested in who he was."

> —Paul, a straight man, after being cut

Lesson: You can't have your cake and eat it, too.

From **THE AMAZING RACE 3**.

When Michael's partner complains he's not doing any of the challenges, he tells her that all of the tasks have involved things he's not good at.

"I can't skydive. I can't kayak. I can't swim. But I can cook."

Lesson: It may be good to know your strengths, but it's even better to get someone else to do the dirty work.

From **EXTREME MAKEOVER**, a show where participants who are deeply unhappy with their appearance and who feel it affects them in a negative way are given a complete makeover, including plastic surgery, a new haircut, clothing, and advice on personal style.

"People have to understand that the most important muscle in changing their body is their mind."

—Michael Thurmond, trainer, working with Dan R., who has just had a makeover

Lesson: Sure, the brain may be strong mentally, but just let it try and bench press two hundred pounds.

From **THE AMAZING RACE 3**.

"I know she's afraid of labels, but I don't mind saying, 'I'm lazy,' and I don't feel like running up a pyramid if I don't think I have to."

> —Michael, admitting that he may not be one of the game's most ambitious contestants

Lesson: Know thyself.

From **THE OSBOURNES**.

"I'm not proud of having a poor education. I'm not proud of being dyslexic and having attention deficit disorder. I'm not proud of being a drug addict/alcoholic. I'm not proud of biting the head off of a bat. I'm not proud of a lot of things, but I'm a real guy with real feelings, and I suppose that kind of scares me sometimes, you know. To be Ozzy Osbourne, it could be worse. I could be Sting."

> —Ozzy, taking stock of his life

Lesson: Count your blessings. No matter how well off or poor you are, it could always be worse.

From **ROOM RAIDERS**, a dating show where a contestant gets to go through the rooms of three members of the opposite sex before meeting them and make a decision on whom to date based on what can be learned about the individuals while rummaging through their stuff.

"The perfect girl for me? Somebody that likes me would be a start. Obviously, she has to be ridiculously good-looking. Let's be honest. I'm a good-looking boy, you know. I'm a catch."

　　—Jason

Lesson: No matter how good- or bad-looking you are, you'll always have better luck with someone who likes you.

From **WHAT NOT TO WEAR**.

"As long as I have hair, I'm happy to have hair. It doesn't matter what it looks like to me."

　　—Dave, a man who likes cheap haircuts, getting ready for a hairstyle makeover

Lesson: It's better to have some hair with no style than no hair with some style.

SEX, DRUGS, AND ROCK AND ROLL

From **THE ANNA NICOLE SHOW**.

"I got my first tattoo, a Playboy bunny, because I was young, dumb, and drunk."

>—Anna Nicole, at the tattoo parlor

Lesson: If you must be young and stupid, try not to get drunk around a tattoo parlor.

From **THE ANNA NICOLE SHOW**.

"We were just having a lot of fun, you know. Lap dance after lap dance and then the bill came and, boom, we were just sort of shocked into sobriety."

>—Howard Stern, Anna's attorney and
>   friend, after an evening at a Vegas strip
>   club

Lesson: It's all fun and games until someone gets the bill.

From **FRATERNITY LIFE**.

"Hello, church. Hello, work. Hello, family. Hello, family friends. Hello, principal. Hello, old teachers. I've learned that going out with a stripper is an incredible amount of fun."

> —Earl, basking in the afterglow of an evening with his stripper girlfriend

Lesson: Some things are self-evident, especially when you're a male virgin in a fraternity.

From **THE OSBOURNES**.

"I'm sorry, I'm not picking up another turd. I'm a rock star."

> —Ozzy, about the problems house-training the dogs

Lesson: Even rock stars have their limits.

From **THE APPRENTICE**, a competition among sixteen budding entrepreneurs vying for a position as president of a company owned by Donald Trump and a $250,000 salary for a year.

"I wouldn't pay $5 for a glass of lemonade, but if it was served by a very pretty girl, you'd be surprised. I might. I'd pay $1 for the lemonade, $4 for the girl."

> —Trump executive vice president George Ross, on one team's decision to increase the price of their potion

Lesson: Sex sells.

From **I'M WITH BUSEY**.

"Gary told me toys would free up my imagination. I told him a six-pack of beer would do the same thing. He didn't go for it. So we went with this toy idea instead."

> —Adam

Lesson: Your imagination will set you free, but so will beer.

From **THE ANNA NICOLE SHOW**.

"I don't want millions of people watching me puke in a hat."

> —Kimmie, at her Halloween birthday party

Lesson: If you don't want an audience watching your every move, either don't drink or don't hang out with someone who has their own reality show.

From **CELEBRITY MOLE YUCATAN**.

"I'll never watch The Cosby Show *the same way again, I'll tell you that."*

> —Mark Curry, after seeing Keisha Knight Pulliam skinny-dipping on the beach.

Lesson: Nudity changes everything.

SHOPPING

From **WHAT NOT TO WEAR**.

*"This just might be the perfect Dave pant of all time.
I've just been told that these are wrinkle-free and stain-
resistant, which means I can spill on myself."*

> —Dave H., a man who doesn't like to spend a
> lot of money on clothes but does like to go
> out drinking, holding a pair of pants at Old
> Navy during his search for a new wardrobe

Lesson: It is possible to have it all.

From **WHAT NOT TO WEAR: BBC**.

*"Unless you're used to it, and unless you've done it before,
and unless you know what you like, it's bloody hard work.
I never thought I'd say that, but spending 2,000 pounds is
hard work."*

> —Meeta, on the difficulty of finding clothes
> that meet the recommendations of the
> show's hosts and match her personality

*Lesson: A fool and his money are soon parted, but
a smart person has a harder time finding ways to
spend.*

From **THE OSBOURNES**.

"The Virgin Mary speaks to me! She says, 'You must go to Tiffany and on the way stop at Cartier.'"

    —Sharon, while shopping

Lesson: To some people, shopping really is a religion.

From **RICH GIRLS**.

"I can't do that. I cannot go shopping and leave my credit card at home. That is so stupid. I'll have an anxiety attack and then form an addiction to my antianxiety pills."

    —Jaime Gleicher, in L.A., on her fear of hitting the stores without credit cards

Lesson: It's important to have a layer of credit to protect you.

STYLE

From ***THE BACHELOR: THE WOMEN TELL ALL***.

"I wish I would not have worn that cream dress on that rose ceremony. If I could go back, I would pick the red, definitely."

—Lee-Ann, talking about the one thing she regrets during her time on the show

Lesson: Not only do clothes make the woman, but the right dress can hide any character flaw.

From ***EXTREME MAKEOVER***.

"Beauty is a little bit uncomfortable."

—Ava T. Shamban, skin specialist

Lesson: It is better to look good than to feel good.

From ***EXTREME MAKEOVER***.

"Fashion is the key. Let fashion lead the way."

—Sam Saboura, fashion stylist

Lesson: Love isn't the answer. Fashion is.

From **QUEER EYE FOR THE STRAIGHT GUY**.

"Guns don't kill people, bad fashion does."

> —Style maven Carson, to Port Authority
> policeman John V., about the importance
> of style

*Lesson: Bad style choices may not be hurting you,
but they're killing your friends.*

From **WHAT NOT TO WEAR**.

*"It's a weird invasion. Someone's telling you that your
clothes suck. It's harsh."*

> —David L., on realizing that his friends
> felt his wardrobe was so awful that they
> nominated him for a televised
> makeover

*Lesson: The truth hurts. It hurts even more when it
comes from close friends.*

From **QUEER EYE FOR THE STRAIGHT GUY**.

"There's a lot of power in a pedicure and a spray-on tan."

    —Kyan, to makeover victim John V.

Lesson: Style can be a tremendous force for good or evil. It's up to us to decide how to use it.

From **WHAT NOT TO WEAR**.

"Who's really to say whether or not my retro is the good kind of retro that's in or the bad kind of retro that's out, 'cause retro is always in somewhere in the world."

    —Ross B., pondering whether he's hopelessly out of fashion or on the edge of the next wave

Lesson: While the style you opt for may currently be in vogue somewhere in the world, if it isn't hip on your block, it's still hopelessly out of date.

From **QUEER EYE FOR THE STRAIGHT GUY**.

"This is really good-looking. Who says there are no gays in the military? Someone designed this uniform."

> —Carson, to former marine Ross M., while looking at the military man's dress uniform

Lesson: Contrary to popular belief, the "don't ask, don't tell" policy does have its benefits.

From **THE REAL WORLD: SEATTLE**.

"Children in Nepal are gorgeous. These are kids that you think you'd see on the covers of Vogue *or* Cosmopolitan *but no, they're not getting any of that attention because that's not how their culture is."*

> —Rebecca, marveling over the little people of Nepal

Lesson: True beauty isn't found on the pages of a magazine.

From **RICH GIRLS**.

"We've seen all the places and we've been to all the boutiques in New York and we know what exists and we know what is good, you know what I mean? But a lot of people don't and they just buy because to someone, clothing is just something that covers them. They don't care what it looks like. They're just pants they need to cover their behind and their penis and their vagina and that's their clothes. You know what I mean? People buy cargo pants in the Midwest not to say you know, like, 'Oh, I could wear these with stilettos and a real cool sexy top,' like I was going to do tonight. They buy them because they have a lot of pockets and they work in the fields and they need them."

—Jaime Gleicher, on those other people

Lesson: Only a select few know the true secrets of fashion. The rest are doomed to wear cargo pants inappropriately.

TECHNOLOGY

From ***THE OSBOURNES***.

On Ozzy's fifty-fourth birthday he gets a BMW with voice-activated commands. The only problem is that the system doesn't understand Ozzy's incoherent ramblings and often supplies words of its own. In one case, it interprets a mumbling as a request to make a phone call.

"I don't want the f - - - ing phone. Will you shut the fuck up? Take five, man. I've got the wife that nags me, now I've got a f - - - ing car that nags me."

— Ozzy, on the difficulty of everyday living in a technological age

Lesson: Know your limitations. And hate them.

From ***I'M WITH BUSEY***.

"Technology is like living with the eyes of a shark. A shark's eyes have no life in them, and the way technology is advancing today, every day there's a new product, every day the prices go up, and guess what? In three weeks' time, maybe two days, maybe a year, maybe half a year,

technology is going to be developed so strict and so refined that it will be able to kill your mother."

—Gary

Lesson: Not all technology is good technology.

From ***THE OSBOURNES.***

"With all these buttons it could give you a f - - - ing blow job. Press 'blow job.'"

> —Ozzy, to his son as he learns how to use a remote control that operates everything in the house

Lesson: Modern technology may have made great advances, but there are some things even the most refined machine hasn't achieved yet.

TOO MUCH INFORMATION

From **SURVIVOR: THE AUSTRALIAN OUTBACK**.

Looking back on a visit with his mother, in which he had an innuendo-filled chat and then cuddled with her in the back of a car, Colby earned the nickname "Oedipus Tex" after talking about their time together:

"It was almost like a conjugal visit if you were a prisoner."

Lesson: Contrary to popular belief, it is possible to share too much.

From **BOY MEETS BOY**.

"All of a sudden I've got this guy Jorge with his hips up in me and I'm like, whoa, bro, what's that back there? It doesn't feel like a belt buckle."

—Dan, a straight guy on a dancing-lesson date

Lesson: If you don't want to know the truth, it's probably best to keep staring straight ahead.

From THE REAL WORLD: SEATTLE.

"I never knew my ass was veiny until I got this picture back."

> —Irene, showing a picture of her colonoscopy to a housemate

Lesson: Modern medical technology may be wonderful, but there's still no cure for sharing too much.

TRAVEL

From **THE AMAZING RACE**.

"I don't think the city is anything special. This is just like being down in SoHo."

> —Kevin, after spending the night on a Paris sidewalk waiting for a tea shop to open

Lesson: Sidewalks are the same all over the world.

From **RICH GIRLS**.

"I wanna, like, run away and be a hippie. I can't, like, be a hippie in New York really because I can't, like, wear bare feet."

> —Ally Hilfiger, considering a change of lifestyle

Lesson: If you are considering an alternate lifestyle, you may actually have to change the way you live.

From **BOY MEETS BOY**.

"I was the lucky one who got the very last position in the horse train. Not only did I get to see the back of everyone's head, but I also got to breathe everyone's dust."

> —Robb, on his experience during a group horse-riding date

Lesson: If you're at the back of the pack, the view never changes.

From **THE AMAZING RACE**.

"That hurt. I think my left testicle is just rolling around in the streets of Beijing."

> —Drew, after hitting a bump while riding in a motorcycle sidecar in China

Lesson: Riding local transportation in foreign countries can be hazardous to your health.

From **NEWLYWEDS: NICK AND JESSICA**.

"I'm not trying to be bitchy, I'm just whiny."

—Jessica, on a camping trip

Lesson: There may be a difference between the two, but neither is much fun on a camping trip.

From **THE AMAZING RACE 2**.

"There's really no way to describe the bus ride except you know how we said that after the island . . . what did I call the island? The island of some sort of torture or terror, it can only get better. We lied. We lied. The bus ride was so horrendous that I wouldn't put my worst enemy in that scenario. . . . It was horrible. There's no room next to the toilet, the smell is coming in, people banging you left and right. And you thought, you know what, I can handle this. We thought it was almost over and I looked at my watch. We were only on it for five hours. And we had to go twenty-two hours."

—Mary, discussing the bus ride from hell

Lesson: Just when you think things can't possibly get any worse, they do.

WINNING AND LOSING

From **BIG BROTHER 2**.

Although some cast members are unhappy with the way Will has lied and stabbed people in the back on his way to winning, he courts their votes with the following spirited defense.

"Say it however you want. If you don't like what happened, then you don't like reality-based TV shows. And if you don't like reality, then you don't like who you are. That's not my fault."

Lesson: Just because someone tries to win by assaulting your self-esteem doesn't mean you have to buy into it. It may be their reality, but it doesn't have to be yours.

From **THE AMAZING RACE**.

"They're doing dances for us, they're singing, they're dancing, and I'm gonna get hit in the eye with these things up here if you don't [change course]."

—Drew, atop a camel, as Kevin leads it into a tree as they arrive in a village

Lesson: Even in the midst of success, there is adversity.

From **AMERICA'S NEXT TOP MODEL**.

When it came time for the judges to interview the three remaining models one more time, Elyse admitted that she originally felt the only thing necessary to becoming a good model was to have a good physical appearance. She had come to believe physical beauty was only part of the package. When asked why she thought she deserved to be America's next top model, she replied, *"I don't think that it's acceptable to say that anyone deserves to win this competition. It's really not a basic human right to get a modeling contract."* She was the next person to be eliminated.

Lesson: Sometimes it's best just to talk about world peace.

From **BIG BROTHER 2**.

"Show me a good loser, and I'll show you a loser."

—Sue, from *Survivor,* on how contestants in the *Big Brother* house should handle themselves during the last few days of the competition

Lesson: It's not whether you win or lose, it's how you win the game that counts.

From **CELEBRITY MOLE YUCATAN**.

"It's not like your farewell or you're voted off, you're exe-cuted. You're done. You're out."

    —Corbin Bernsen, talking about the show's choice of phrase to describe what happens when a player is eliminated from the game

Lesson: Execution is final.

From **SURVIVOR: PEARL ISLANDS**.

"I'm not happy about playing this game as well as I did and not being one of the final two. I feel that the strongest player in this game made it as far as he could make it and that there are two people that don't deserve to be there. Johnny Fairplay is going to have a fun time at the tribal council at night. The one thing I can promise tonight is that I won't play fair."

    —Johnny Fairplay

Lesson: Sore losers are so unattractive.

From *QUEER EYE FOR THE STRAIGHT GUY*.

"I consider myself a very witty person, but I've got to tell you with the gay men, it don't work. It don't work. I am. If I were gay, I'd be a very quiet gay person."

    —Steven S.

Lesson: There will always be someone funnier, prettier, richer, or smarter. The true measure of a man is how he accepts defeat.

WORK

From **THE REAL WORLD: LAS VEGAS**.

When Brynn learns about her new job planning events at a local nightclub, she is less than happy because it isn't exactly what she wants.

"Personally, I only like to dance. I don't even know if I can dance on this job."

Lesson: It's important to have your priorities straight when starting a job. If you're not doing what you want to do, why bother?

From **THE RESTAURANT**.

On the night of the soft launch, Rocco tells his brother, *"It's cool you know? It's like a little dream come true, you know? You know, like, we grew up kind of ashamed of being Italian and it's, like, finally I'm comfortable enough to be proud of it."*

Lesson: It's, you know, easy to be proud of your ethnic heritage when you can, like, make money off of it.

From **1900 HOUSE**.

"I want to be a benevolent employer. I suppose I'll be giving her cups of tea, free access to the outside toilet. I mean, what else can I give her? There aren't really a lot of perks to this job. As much fluff [dust] as you can take home."

—Joyce, on hiring a maid

Lesson: "Fringe benefits" is a relative term.

From **FAMILY BUSINESS**, a look at a family that owns a company specializing in adult-entertainment videos.

"Sex is supposed to be relaxing, unless of course it's your job."

—Adam Glasser, adult-film producer

Lesson: Work takes all the fun out of everything.

From **FAKING IT**.

"Look, I don't want to undermine your confidence too much but you're not going to be able to get away with leaving

critics alone with, or divas alone with something like this and have them say, 'You're an undiscovered genius,' because demonstrably, you're not."

> —Art critic David Lee, reviewing Paul's works
> of art just days before his gallery premiere

Lesson: A good critic should tell it like it is so artists can learn from their mistakes.

From **AVERAGE JOE**.

"Some people want to be doctors, some people want to be lawyers. I want to be a weatherman. I even have a name picked out. Jason Storm."

> —Good-looking guy Jason, to Malena

Lesson: No matter how modest, it's good to have a career goal.

From **FAKING IT**.

"He's put it in an art form. I do this every day. When I'm painting a door externally quite often flies will stick to the

paint. I'm constantly killing them. I never looked at them as being an art form. I just felt sorry for them."

—Paul, the house painter, after seeing an art-
work with dead butterflies on it and being
told it reflects the artist's fascination with
death and beauty

Lesson: One man's art is another man's drop cloth.

THE LONG KISS
GOOD-BYE

From **THE BACHELOR**.

"I honestly want you to know that any time, any place, anywhere, I would never not want to get to know you even better than I have, but I feel like I'd be being dishonest with you if I said that I didn't think truthfully that everything that you want and everything that you're looking for, you'd be compromising by being with me. It's me not knowing my time line on things."

> —Bob the Bachelor, explaining to Mary why he eliminated her from the competition for his affections

Lesson: No matter how you slice it, it's not you, it's me.

From **THE BACHELOR: THE WOMEN TELL ALL**.

"I don't know what happened. I mean, I think that something else happened that I don't know about. If one of the girls told Bob something bad about me and he listened to it enough to cut me tonight then, yuck, grow up!"

> —Lee-Ann, after being eliminated from the competition for Bachelor Bob's affections

Lesson: It's not me, it's you.

ABOUT THE AUTHOR

David Volk is a silly man who likes to keep the pot
stirred. A newspaper reporter–turned–freelance writer
and humorist, he enjoys looking for urban adventures, odd experiences, and kitschy places that locals
overlook.

As a member of the Seattle Cacophony Society,
he participated in street theater events such as "The
Bob Dylan Holiday Choir" and regularly organized
"The Inanimate Object Bungee Jump and Donner
Party Memorial (Tastes Like Chicken) Barbecue." He
wrote and performed the one-man comedy show
"Baggage" at the Seattle International Fringe Festival
and has done humor commentaries for a local
National Public Radio station.

Volk also writes regular humorous rants on his
Web site at www.davidvolk.com and sends them out
to subscribers on his rant list.

His work has appeared in national, regional, and
local publications including the *Chicago Tribune*,
Alaska Airlines Magazine, *Seattle Homes and Lifestyles*,

Seattle Magazine, *Koi World*, and the guidebook *Best Places Seattle*.

He also has a serious side but often has trouble locating it.

When he isn't watching reality television, he can usually be found roaming around Seattle, having urban adventures, working on travel pieces, writing magazine articles, or hanging out with his wife, Cindy.